3. The last photo taken will be shown (if not, select it with the Quick Control Dial). Press SET, then select OK.

4. Select MENU > Shooting (Screen 4) > White Balance, and then select the Custom White Balance icon.

COLOR SPACE

MENU > Shooting (Screen 4) > Color Space

sRGB: Smaller color space. Best when images are used directly from camera.

Adobe RGB: Larger color space. Best used when images will be edited with post-processing software.

HIGHLIGHT ALERT (BLINKIES)

MENU > Playback (Screen 5) > Highlight Alert

Select Enable so that clipped highlights will blink, alerting you to possible overexposure when playing back images. To obtain more detail in those areas, adjust exposure settings or exposure compensation and shoot again.

NOISE REDUCTION

MENU > Shooting (Screen 5) > Long Exposure Noise Reduction

Reduces noise in images with shutter speeds of 1 second or longer. Doubles time needed to save image to memory card. Choices are Auto, Enable, and Disable. Auto is usually the best choice.

MENU > Shooting (Screen 5) > High ISO Speed NR

Reduces noise in images taken at high ISO settings. Use Standard for default, Low for less noise reduction, and High for more noise reduction. Multi Shot Noise Reduction applies noise reduction with higher image quality than High by combining four photos into a single JPEG image. Multi Shot Noise Reduction is not available when shooting RAW or RAW+JPEG.

AUTO ISO

MENU > Shooting (Screen 2) > ISO Speed Settings

Within the ISO Speed Settings, you can select Auto for the ISO Speed, then use the Auto Range option to set the minimum and maximum ISO settings to define the range that the camera can use. You can also set the Minimum Shutter Speed to ensure that the camera does not lower the shutter speed too much; this helps reduce camera shake and blurry images.

EXPOSURE BRACKETING

You can bracket a set of three exposures up to +/-3 stops in 1/3-stop increments:

1. Select MENU > Shooting (Screen 2) > Expo.comp./ AEB.
2. Set the Bracketing range by turning the Main dial.
3. If desired, set the exposure compensation amount by turning the Quick Control Dial. Press SET.
4. Take the pictures, and three bracketed shots will be created. (If you're in Single shooting drive mode, take three pictures to create the bracketed sequence. If you're in a Continuous shooting drive mode, the three shots will be taken together when you press and hold the Shutter button.)

Note: Bracketing will remain on until you set the Bracketing range back to 0.

WIRELESS CONNECTION

Install the Camera Connect app on your smartphone and pair it with the EOS R7.

This will allow you to view and transfer images to your smartphone, see the Live View image on your smartphone, and even shoot remotely from your smartphone.

RESET CAMERA

MENU > Set-Up (Screen 6) > Reset Camera

Select Basic Settings to restore the default settings for the shooting functions and menu settings. Select Other Settings to choose individual settings to reset to their default settings.

05 STEP-BY-STEP SHOOTING INSTRUCTIONS

MULTIPLE EXPOSURES

Create in-camera multiple exposures:

1. Select MENU > Shooting (Screen 6) > Multiple Exposure, and select Enable.
2. Choose a Multiple Exposure Control option:

   Additive: The exposure of each image is added cumulatively.

   Average: Based on the number of exposures you set (next step), negative exposure compensation is added automatically as you shoot to achieve a standard overall exposure.

   Bright: Retains brightest portion of images.

   Dark: Retains darkest portion of images.
3. Set the number of exposures you'd like to combine, then press SET.
4. Set a Continue Multiple Exposure option:

   1 Shot Only: Shoot just one multiple exposure.

   Continuously: Continue shooting multiple exposures until you disable the feature.

5. Shoot all of the exposures to combine into one multiple exposure. ***Note:*** As you shoot, press the Playback button to show the current exposure and how the images look merged together. Pressing the Erase Button allows you to Return to previous screen, Undo last image (deletes the last image and allows you to retake it), Save and exit (saves the photos you have already taken and exits the Multiple Exposure shooting mode), or Exit without saving (exits the Multiple Exposure shooting mode without saving an image).

HDR HDR

Combine three images to reduce the contrast and improve tonal range. The Canon EOS R7 generates one JPEG or HEIF image as the resulting HDR image:

1. Select MENU > Shooting (Screen 2) > HDR Mode.
2. Choose the dynamic range you want:

   Auto: Sets the dynamic range automatically depending on the scene's tonal range.

   +/–1, +/–2, or +/–3: The higher the number, the wider the dynamic range of the image will be.

3. Set Limit Max Brightness to Disable (where the max brightness is not limited) or 1000 nits (where the brightness will be limited to appoximately 1000 nits).

4. Select an option for Continuous HDR:

   1 Shot Only: You'll only shoot one HDR image.

   Every Shot: You'll keep shooting HDR images until you disable HDR shooting by selecting MENU > Shooting (Screen 2) > HDR Mode > Disable HDR.

5. Select the Auto Image Align setting:

   Enable: Choose this if you're shooting handheld.

   Disable: Choose if you're shooting on a tripod.

6. Determine if you'd like to save all the images that you shoot or just the resulting HDR image with the Save Source Images option.

7. Take the picture.

TIME-LAPSE MOVIES

Create a time-lapse movie in-camera:

1. Select MENU > Shooting (Screen 5) > Time-Lapse Movie, and then choose Enable.
2. Select Interval and enter both the shooting duration and the movie playback duration.
3. Set the No. of Shots you'd like to take for the time-lapse movie.
4. Select the desired Movie Recording Size (4K or Full HD).
5. Select Auto Exposure to choose the shooting method:

   Fixed 1st Frame: The first shot is metered, then all subsequent shots match that first shot's exposure.

   Each Frame: Each frame is metered and shot separately.
6. In the Screen Auto Off option, choose Disable to have the image displayed (though the screen will automatically turn off 30 minutes after the time-lapse shooting begins); choose Enable to have the screen turn off 10 seconds after the time-lapse shooting begins. ***Note:*** You can press the INFO button at any time during time-lapse shooting to turn the screen on and off.

7. Choose whether you'd like to hear a beep after every image is captured (Beep per Image Taken).

8. Once all settings are selected, press MENU to turn off the menu screen.

9. A message will come on screen prompting you to take a test shot. Press OK, and take a test shot or two to make sure the correct focus and exposure are set.

10. Press the Movie Shooting button, then press the Shutter button to start shooting the time-lapse movie.

06 TYPICAL SHOOTING SCENARIOS

SHOOTING SCENARIO
PORTRAIT

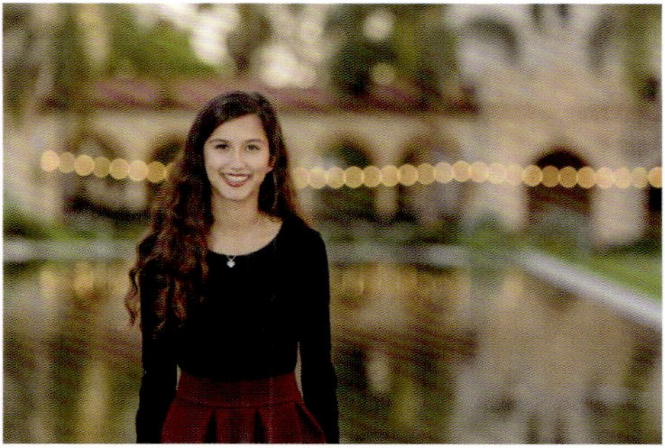

KEY PRINCIPLES

- The key to a portrait like this is shallow depth of field. So shoot in **APERTURE PRIORITY (Av)** mode and start with the lowest aperture your lens offers (such as **f/2.8** or **f/4**).
- Remember to **focus on the eyes**.
- If the image is too dark or too light, use **EXPOSURE COMPENSATION** to adjust the brightness level.

- If the image is blurry from a slow shutter speed, **raise the ISO** to increase your sensor's sensitivity to light, thus allowing for a faster shutter speed.
- Remember to use a **focal length of 50mm or greater** so that you don't distort your subject's face.

SHOOTING SCENARIO
GROUP PORTRAIT

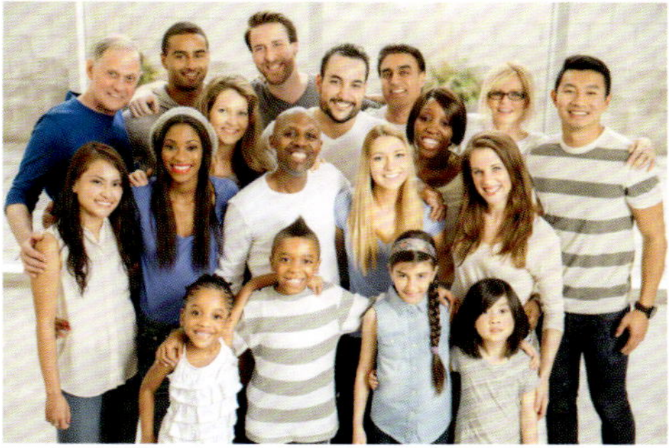

KEY PRINCIPLES

- In order to get everyone in focus, you need a deep depth of field. So shoot in **APERTURE PRIORITY (Av)** mode and set the aperture between **f/8–f/16**.

- **Focus on the person in the middle of the group.** Check the focus by using the LCD screen. View it at 100% and check faces in the front and back rows. If anyone is out of focus, use a smaller aperture for deeper depth of field.
- Use **EVALUATIVE METERING** to account for the light in the entire scene.
- **Arrange the group so they can all see you** (and you can see them).
- Use **EXPOSURE COMPENSATION** if the image is too bright or too dark.
- If image is blurry, **raise the ISO** to allow the camera to use a faster shutter speed.

SHOOTING SCENARIO

LANDSCAPE

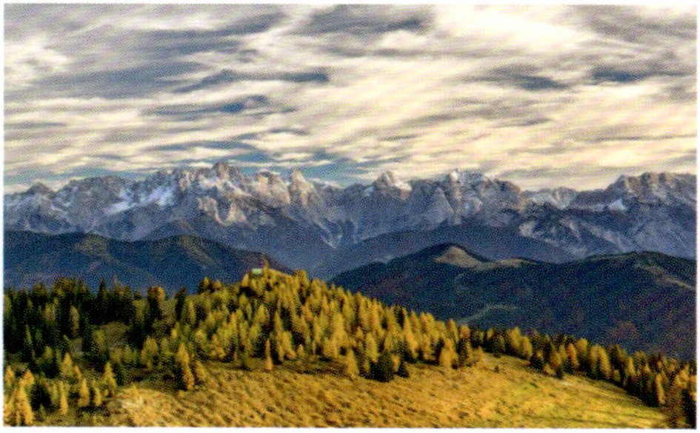

KEY PRINCIPLES

- Shoot in **APERTURE PRIORITY (Av)** mode to control depth of field, and start with **f/16** to ensure deep depth of field.
- **Use a tripod** to eliminate camera movement. Whenever your camera is on a tripod, also make sure that any **IMAGE STABILIZATION** is turned off.
- Use **EVALUATIVE METERING** and **ONE-SHOT AF** focus mode.
- **Set the ISO to a low setting (100–200)** to avoid any digital noise.
- Shoot in **RAW** so that you have the most available information when editing later.
- Consider **BRACKETING** your exposures.

SHOOTING SCENARIO

FREEZE ACTION

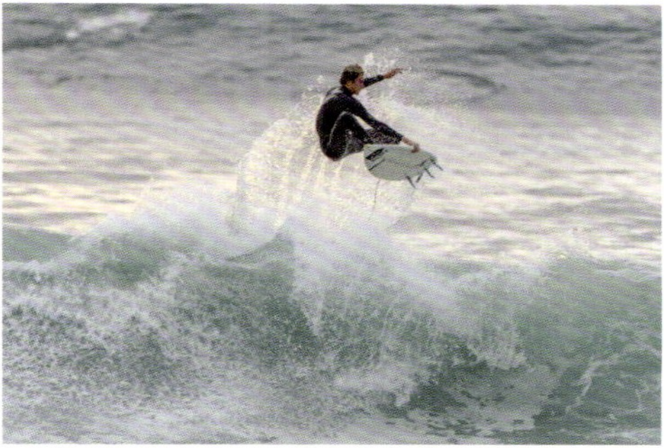

KEY PRINCIPLES

- Use **SHUTTER PRIORITY (Tv)** mode and set the shutter speed to a value that will freeze the action. The appropriate shutter speed depends on your subject and its movement, but could be anywhere between **1/500–1/4000 sec**.
- Use **SERVO** autofocus so that the camera keeps focusing as the subject moves.
- If the image is dark or blurry, **raise the ISO or try AUTO ISO** to automatically have the camera adjust the ISO as needed.

SHOWING MOTION—PANNING

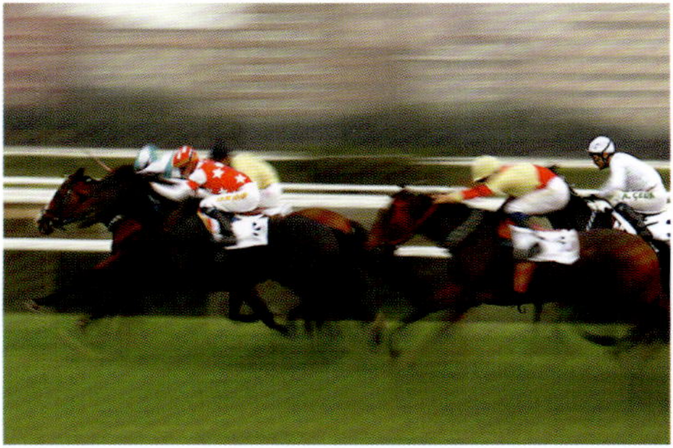

KEY PRINCIPLES

- Shoot in **SHUTTER PRIORITY (Tv)** mode and use a slow-enough shutter speed to allow for the subject to move during the exposure.
- **Follow the subject** across the frame as you shoot.
- Use **SERVO** autofocus, as well as the **EXPAND AF AREA** focus mode to ensure the camera focuses on the subject.

SHOOTING SCENARIO

LOW-LIGHT ACTION

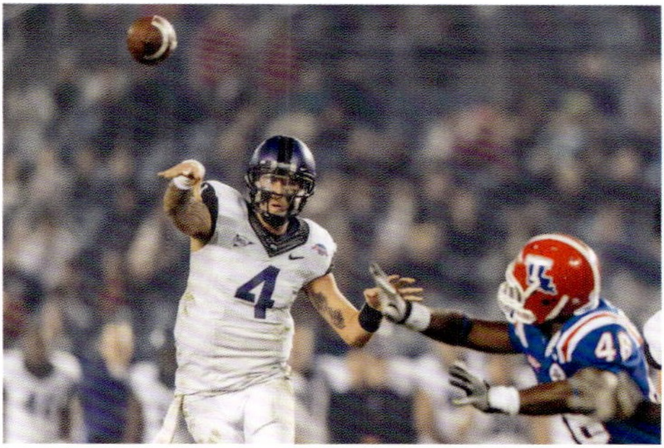

KEY PRINCIPLES

- Shoot in **APERTURE PRIORITY (Av)** mode and use a wide aperture such as **f/2.8 or f/4**.
- Use **PARTIAL METERING** and meter on the subject's face.
- Use **SERVO** autofocus and **1-POINT AF** (a single focus point).
- **Set the ISO to 1600 or higher**, depending on the amount of available light.
- If the image is blurry, **increase the ISO** to allow for a faster shutter speed.

SHOOTING SCENARIO

LONG EXPOSURE

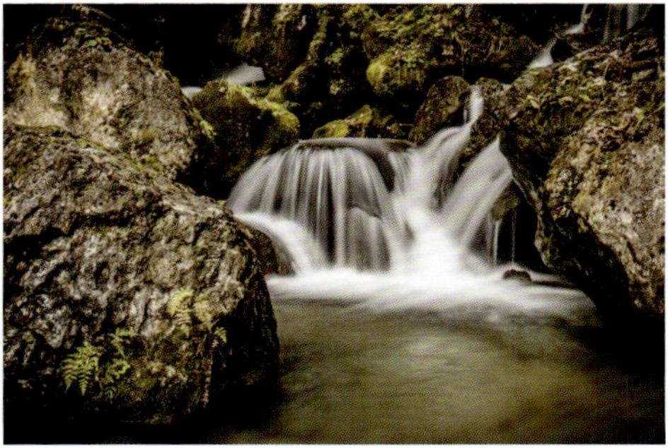

KEY PRINCIPLES

- Use **MANUAL** or **BULB** shooting mode so you can use a long shutter speed.
- **Use a tripod** to keep the camera stable. **Turn off any IMAGE STABILIZATION**.
- Use the **ONE-SHOT AF** focus mode, or try manual focus if the camera is having a hard time locking on focus.
- **Use a low ISO** (100–400) and shoot RAW to ensure a high-quality file.
- Use a **cable release** with a lock to avoid touching (shaking) the camera.

SHOOTING SCENARIO
MACRO/CLOSE-UP

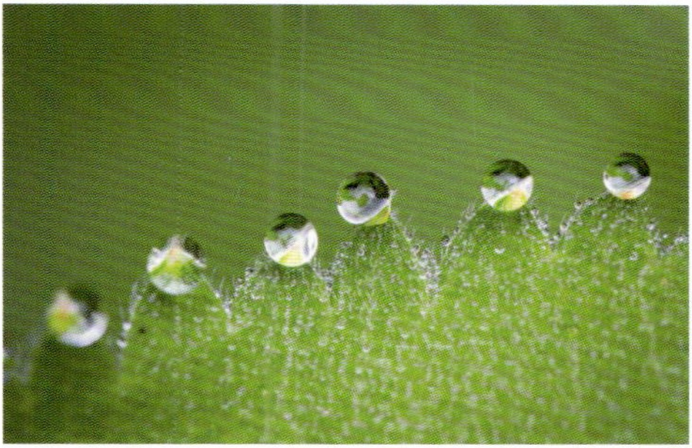

KEY PRINCIPLES

- Shoot in **APERTURE PRIORITY (Av)** mode and **use a small aperture** to ensure you achieve enough depth of field (this image was shot at f/13).
- Use **EVALUATIVE METERING** to analyze the light in the entire frame.
- A **tripod** is very useful for keeping the camera steady.
- Use **MANUAL FOCUS** and **Magnified View** to confirm your focus is tack-sharp.
- Try using a dedicated **macro lens** or **close-up filters** to make sure you can achieve sharp focus when you're so close to the subject.

CANON EOS R50

POCKET GUIDE

TABLE OF CONTENTS